THE MOON

BY HOLLY DUHIG

©2017
Book Life
King's Lynn
Norfolk PE30 4LS

ISBN: 978-1-78637-200-0

Written by:
Holly Duhig
Edited by:
Charlie Ogden
Designed by:
Danielle Rippengill

A catalogue record for this book
is available from the British Library

PHOTO CREDITS

Abbreviations: l-left, r-right, b-bottom, t-top, c-centre, m-middle.

CONTENTS

Words that look like *this* are explained in the glossary on page 31.

WHAT IS A MOON?

A moon is an object in space that moves around a planet. This movement is called orbiting. Orbiting is where an object in space makes a regular path around another, larger object. Anything that orbits something else in space is called a satellite. Moons can be any size, but they must be smaller than the object that they orbit around.

Scientists send *man-made* satellites into orbit and use them to take photographs of things in space. Moons are *natural* satellites that are usually made from rock.

Jupiter's biggest moon, Ganymede, is bigger than Mercury. However, as it orbits a planet, it is still considered a moon. Moons are usually made from rock, but many, such as Jupiter's moon Europa, are also made of ice.

Some planets, like Saturn, have rings around them that are made up of pieces of rock and ice that are orbiting the planet. Even though these are natural objects that orbit a planet, they do not count as moons. This is because they have not come together to form one single, large object.

THE MOON

Planet Earth has one moon. The Earth is only about four times wider than the Moon. The Moon looks much smaller than this in the sky, but that's only because it's far away.

The Moon is 384,400 kilometres away from the Earth!

Sometimes we can see the Moon very faintly in the daytime.

The Moon shines at night because the Sun's light is reflecting off its surface. This happens during the daytime too, but we can't see it because our sky is lit up by the Sun and the light bouncing off the Moon gets lost.

WHAT IS IT LIKE TO WALK ON THE MOON?

There is very little gravity on the Moon. The Moon has weaker gravity than the Earth because it is smaller. This means if you dropped a pen on the Moon, it would take longer to fall to the ground than it would on Earth.

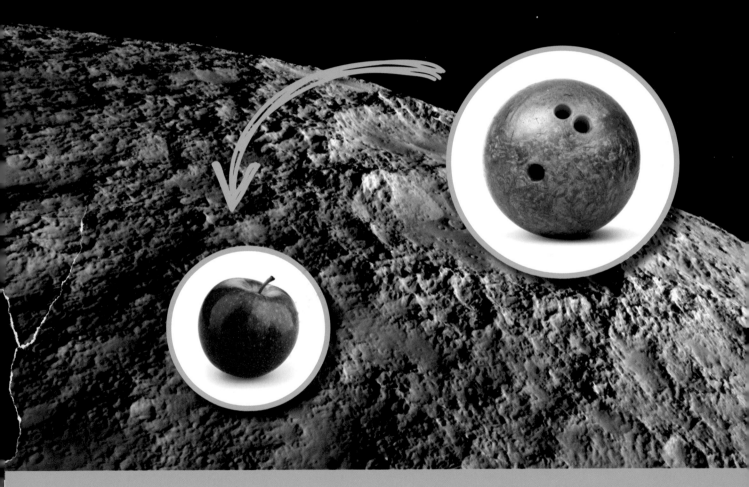

Walking on the Moon is difficult because you weigh less on the Moon. On the Moon, a 16-pound (7.26 kg) bowling ball would weigh about the same as an apple would on Earth. **Astronauts** weigh less on the Moon, so they have to wear heavy boots that allow them to walk around normally.

HOW DID THE MOON GET THERE?

When astronauts land on the Moon, they often collect rocks and bring them back to Earth for scientists to look at. Studying these rocks has led scientists to believe that most of the rock that makes up the Moon used to be part of the Earth.

Scientists think that billions of years ago, when planet Earth was very young, it was hit by a huge **meteorite** the size of Mars. Scientists believe this would have sent pieces of rock from the Earth flying into space. These rocks would then have begun orbiting the planet in a ring. That's right! Planet Earth might have had rings just like Saturn. Over time, gravity would have caused these rocks to come together and form one object – the Moon.

WHAT IS THE MOON MADE OF?

Crust
70km

Mantle
2890km

Iron Core
3470km

Ancient *astronomers* used to think the Moon's dark patches were seas.

Crust
60km

Mantle
1000km

Iron Core
360km

If you look at the Moon in the night sky, you will notice it has many dark patches. These patches are flat low-lands called lunar maria. They are dark because they don't reflect the Sun very well. They exist because the Moon was home to many active volcanoes when it was young. The lava that was produced when these erupted wore away parts of the Moon's surface.

HOW THE MOON AFFECTS US

TIDES

The Moon's gravity is strong enough to affect water on Earth. As the Moon moves around the Earth, the water on Earth slightly bulges towards it. This doesn't happen in small bodies of water, but in large bodies of water, like the ocean, the effect is very clear. We call this movement of the ocean 'the tide'.

There are two high and two low tides each day.

High Tide

Earth

High Tide

Moon

The Earth's gravity is stronger than the Moon's, which is why the oceans don't fly off the surface of the planet when the Moon comes by. As the Earth turns away from the Moon, it becomes harder for the Moon to pull on the oceans and the sea level drops again. This is called low tide.

MYTHS AND LEGENDS

People in the past often did not understand what the Moon was or where it came from. Many cultures saw the Moon as a goddess. They made up stories to explain what the Moon was, what powers she had and where she came from. In Greek mythology, the goddess of the Moon was called Selene and in Roman mythology, her name was Luna.

Native American tribespeople believed the Sun and the Moon were husband and wife and that the stars were their children. They also believed the Sun wanted to eat his children so they hid from him in the daytime but appeared with their mother, the Moon, at night while the Sun was sleeping.

PHASES OF THE MOON

Just like on Earth, one side of the Moon is always lit by the Sun. How much of this lit-up side we see depends on the position of the Earth. Sometimes we will only see a thin sliver of the Moon, but other times we can see a full moon.

The different shapes that the Moon appears to be are called the phases of the Moon. There are eight phases, each of which has its own name.

Waxing Gibbous

First Quarter

Full M

Waxing Crescent

A new moon is the first phase of the Moon and it is not visible from Earth. This is because, during a new moon, the Sun is almost directly behind the Moon and is only lighting up the side facing it. This leaves the side of the Moon facing Earth in total darkness.

Each day, the Moon moves a little farther around the Earth and is lit from a slightly different angle by the Sun. Over the 29 days of the Moon's orbit, it is lit from every different angle, which creates the changing phases of the Moon.

When the Sun lights up more of the Moon each night, the Moon is said to be waxing, and when the Sun lights up less of the Moon each night, the Moon is said to be waning.

loon

Waning Gibbous

Last Quarter

Waning Crescent

Occasionally there will be two full moons in one month. Because it takes 29 days for the Moon to complete its cycle, if a full moon appears on the first day of a new month, there will be another full moon on the 30th day of the month. This happens very rarely – about once every two to three years. The second full moon in a month is called a blue moon, which is why the saying 'once in a blue moon' is used to describe things that happen very rarely.

ECLIPSES

LUNAR ECLIPSES

Lunar eclipses happen when the Sun, Earth and Moon are directly in line with each other. When this happens, the Earth blocks the sunlight from reaching the Moon and makes it appear dark orange.

Lunar eclipses are also called blood moons.

A very small amount of the Sun's light is bent around the Earth and reflected off the Moon's surface. This is what turns the Moon a dark orange colour. Lunar eclipses are safe to look at without eye protection.

SOLAR ECLIPSES

A solar eclipse happens when the Moon moves between the Sun and the Earth. This stops light from the Sun reaching the Earth.

You should never look directly at a solar eclipse because, even though the Sun looks darker, its rays can still damage your eyes.

The part of Earth that is directly in the Moon's shadow will experience a total eclipse, where the whole sky goes dark and the Sun appears to be blotted out. During a solar eclipse, the Moon looks like a black disk and we can see the Sun's corona shining around it. The corona is the outer layer of *gases* on the Sun that we normally can't see because the rest of the Sun's light overpowers it. The corona appears like a red ring in the sky.

THE MOON'S FAR SIDE

Although the Moon *rotates*, we can only ever see one side of the Moon from Earth. This is because it takes the Moon the same amount of time to spin once on its axis as it does for it to orbit the Earth. This means that the same side of the Moon is always facing Earth. This effect is called *tidal locking*.

The side of the Moon we don't see is often called the 'dark side of the Moon', but it is not actually dark. It gets just as much sunlight as the side that faces Earth. During a new moon (when the Moon appears dark from the Earth) the far side of the Moon is still being lit up by the Sun. Astronauts have now seen the far side of the Moon by orbiting it in spacecraft.

Surprisingly, the 'dark' side of the Moon is lighter than the side we can see. There are many deep   on the side of the Moon that faces the Earth. These can cast shadows and create dark patches. The so-called 'dark side' has less of these shadowy valleys so it reflects more of the Sun's light.

The first photographs of the far side of the Moon were taken by a satellite in 1959, but the first time it was seen by human eyes was during the Apollo 8 mission in 1968.

LANDING ON THE MOON

FIRST MAN ON THE MOON

In 1969 people landed on the Moon for the first time.
The first man to set foot on the Moon was the American astronaut, Neil Armstrong.
Armstrong was joined by the astronaut Buzz Aldrin just minutes later.

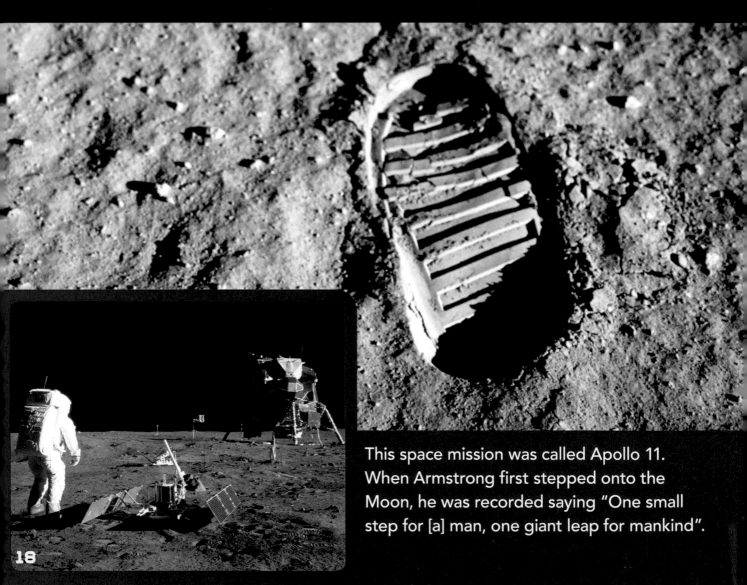

This space mission was called Apollo 11. When Armstrong first stepped onto the Moon, he was recorded saying "One small step for [a] man, one giant leap for mankind".

Before landing, the astronauts were worried that the Moon's surface might be covered in a thick dust that their spacecraft would sink into when it landed. Luckily, this wasn't the case. Once on the Moon, Armstrong and Aldrin spent time exploring the surface and collecting rocks. They also left an American flag on the Moon.

When they got back to Earth, Armstrong and the rest of the astronauts were not allowed to go anywhere for 18 days. This was because, back then, scientists were not sure what was on the Moon and they were worried that the astronauts might bring back bacteria that could make people very sick.

FUTURE OF THE MOON

So, what is the future of the Moon? People have always dreamed of being able to live on the Moon, but is it even possible? One thing is for sure, there would be plenty of changes that we would have to get used to.

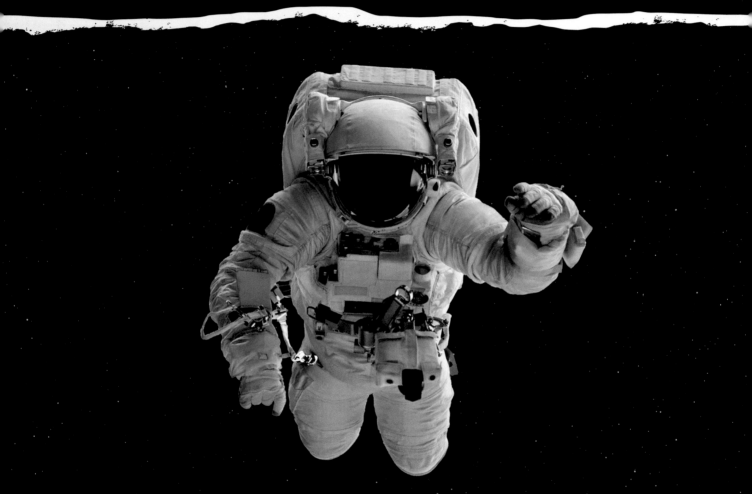

If you wanted to live on the Moon, you would have to get used to wearing a space suit just so that you could breathe. You would also have to get used to very hot days and very cold nights. Daytime on the Moon can reach 123°C and drop to about -150°C at night. These days and nights can last as long as 14 days on Earth. This is because the Moon spins 14 times slower than the Earth, which makes its days 14 times longer.

You would also need your spacesuit to protect you from the Sun's rays. On Earth, our thick   of gases protects us from being burnt by these rays. However, because the Moon has very little atmosphere, your skin would quickly get burnt if you weren't wearing a spacesuit.

After spending a long time in space, astronauts often have to be carried off the space shuttle when they return to Earth because their muscles are not used to the gravity.

Living with weaker gravity would also weaken your muscles. On Earth, gravity forces you to use your muscles. Every time you lift your feet to walk or lift a heavy object, you are using your muscles to defy gravity. On the Moon, you and everything you lift would be much lighter and you would lose your strength very quickly.

MOONS IN THE SOLAR SYSTEM

Scientists are still working out exactly how many moons each planet has. Some planets, like Jupiter, Saturn and Neptune, may have moons that we currently don't know about.

0   0   1   2   67

The Solar System is home to many moons besides our own. In fact, most of the planets in our Solar System have more moons than us, except for Mercury and Venus which have none. This is because Mercury and Venus are too close to the Sun and if they had any moons they would be pulled away by the Sun's gravity. Not all moons are like our own. Some are covered in ice, others are covered in volcanoes and some have thick atmospheres and huge oceans, just like Earth.

The moons in the Solar System have been given some strange names. Mars's moons, Phobos and Deimos, are named after two brothers from Greek mythology whose names mean fear and terror. Many of Uranus's 27 moons are named after characters from the plays of William Shakespeare, a celebrated English playwright. One of Uranus's moons is named Juliet after the leading lady in Shakespeare's famous play, Romeo and Juliet.

Deimos

Phobos

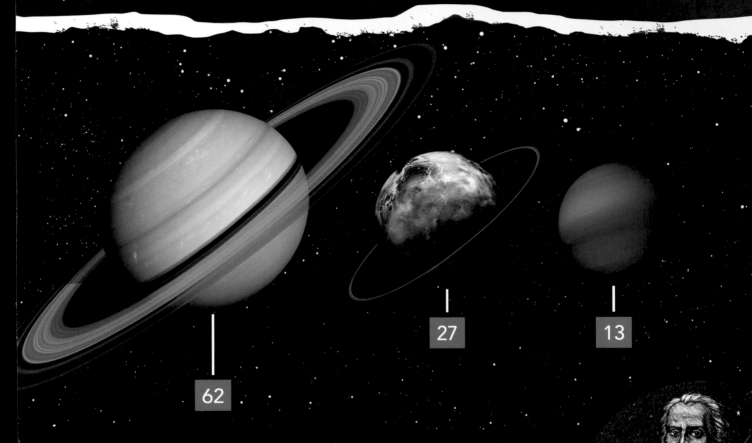

62

27

13

Four of the moons in the Solar System were discovered as early as 1610 by the famous astronomer Galileo Galilei. They are called the Galilean moons. Galileo was only able to discover these moons thanks to his own invention – the telescope!

GALILEAN MOONS

Jupiter has 67 moons. All four of the Galilean moons orbit Jupiter.

GANYMEDE

Ganymede orbits Jupiter about once every seven days. It is the largest moon in the Solar System. It is bigger than both Mercury and the dwarf planet Pluto.

EUROPA

Europa is the smoothest body in the Solar System because its surface is covered in ice. Below this surface, Europa is thought to have a deep ocean. Many scientists believe that simple forms of life might live in these oceans, but it is very difficult for us to know for sure.

IO

Io was the first moon to be discovered after Earth's own moon. It has more volcanoes than anywhere else in the Solar System, some of which are taller than Mount Everest. It is home to over 400 active volcanoes, which makes its surface very rough.

CALLISTO

Callisto is covered in more craters than any other object in the Solar System. Like Europa, it is probably home to an ocean under its surface. Its many craters contrast with its frosty highlands and gives Callisto a glittery appearance.

SATURN'S MOONS

Saturn is the sixth planet from the Sun and has 62 moons orbiting it. Two of these moons orbit in between Saturn's rings!

TITAN

In 1655, Titan became the first of Saturn's moons to be discovered. Titan is the only moon with a dense, cloudy atmosphere like the one on Earth.

ENCELADUS

Enceladus is one of the moons that orbits Saturn from inside its rings. Its surface is made of ice, which reflects the Sun's light so well that it is the most reflective place in the Solar System.

HYPERION

One of Saturn's moons, Hyperion, has a very unusual orbit. It speeds up and slows down depending on how close it is to Titan. Titan's much stronger gravity causes the moons to speed up and slow down as they pass each other.

IAPETUS

Iapetus is a moon that really does have a dark side! While one side is light and reflective, the other side is very dark. Scientists are unsure why this is, but one theory suggests that it is the result of an asteroid smashing into Iapetus. The side of the moon that got hit was covered by dark debris from the asteroid, which has become darker as it has absorbed the Sun's heat.

MARVELLOUS MOONS

Other planets in the Solar System also boast some incredible moons!

PHOBOS

Phobos is the larger of Mars's two moons and it is moving closer and closer to its planet. One day it will crash into Mars or be broken up by Mars's gravity.

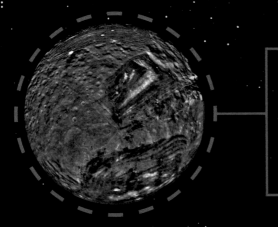

MIRANDA

Miranda is one of Uranus's moons. It is home to Verona Rupes, which, at a height of 20 kilometres, is the steepest cliff in the Solar System.

TRITON

Neptune's moon, Triton, is the only large moon in the Solar System to have a retrograde orbit. This means it orbits in the opposite direction to Neptune's rotation.

CHARON

Even dwarf planets can have moons. Because Pluto is so small, its biggest moon, Charon, is half its size. This makes it the biggest moon, relative to the size of the planet it orbits, in the Solar System.

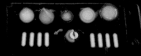

QUICK QUIZ

How many kilometres away from the Earth is the Moon?

What are the dark patches on the Moon called?

How many high tides are there each day?

Who was the Greek goddess of the Moon?

What is a waxing moon?

Why can we only see one side of the Moon?

What year was the first Moon landing?

How hot can the Moon get during its daytime?

How many moons does Uranus have?

Which four moons are the Galilean moons?

Which of Saturn's moons has a dense, cloudy atmosphere?

What is the name of Pluto's biggest moon?

GLOSSARY

ASTEROID	a rocky and irregularly shaped object that orbits around the Sun
ASTRONOMERS	people who study the universe and objects in space
ATMOSPHERE	the mixture of gases that surround some objects in space
BACTERIA	microscopic living things that can cause diseases
GASES	air-like substances that expand freely to fill any space available
GRAVITY	the force that attracts celestial bodies together and increases in strength as a body's mass increases
MAN-MADE	not natural, made by humans
METEORITE	a piece of rock that successfully enters a planet's atmosphere without being destroyed
MYTHOLOGY	collections of stories that belong to a particular culture
NATURAL	found in nature, not man-made
ORBITING	moving around an object in space in a circular path
PLAYWRIGHT	someone who writes plays
ROTATES	turns around a central point or axis
SATELLITE	any object in space that orbits another object
SEA LEVEL	the level of the sea's surface
TIDAL LOCKING	when the time it takes for a moon to rotate is the same as the time it takes to complete its orbit
TIDES	the rising and falling of sea levels
VALLEYS	long, narrow and deep grooves in the land, usually between hills or mountains

INDEX